strange attractor

BOOKS BY ANNE SIMPSON

POETRY
Is
Quick
Loop
Light Falls Through You

NOVELS
Falling
Canterbury Beach

ESSAYS
The Marram Grass: Poetry & Otherness

strange attractor

strange attractor

poems

Anne Simpson

McCLELLAND & STEWART

Copyright © 2019 by Anne Simpson

McClelland & Stewart and colophon are registered trademarks of Penguin Random House Canada Limited.

All rights reserved. The use of any part of this publication reproduced, transmitted in any form or by any means, electronic, mechanical, photocopying, recording, or otherwise, or stored in a retrieval system, without the prior written consent of the publisher—or, in case of photocopying or other reprographic copying, a licence from the Canadian Copyright Licensing Agency—is an infringement of the copyright law.

Library and Archives Canada Cataloguing in Publication

Title: Strange attractor / Anne Simpson.
Names: Simpson, Anne, author.
Description: Poems.
Identifiers: Canadiana (print) 20190098767 | Canadiana (ebook) 20190098775 |
ISBN 9780771007125 (softcover) | ISBN 9780771007132 (EPUB)
Classification: LCC PS8587.I54533 S77 2019 | DDC C811/.6—dc23

Published simultaneously in the United States of America by McClelland & Stewart, a division of Penguin Random House Canada Limited, a Penguin Random House Company

Library of Congress Control Number is available upon request

ISBN: 978-0-7710-0712-5
ebook ISBN: 978-0-7710-0713-2

Typeset in Centaur by M&S, Toronto

Book design: Rachel Cooper
Cover art: ©PASIEKA/SPL/Getty Images

Printed and bound in Canada

McClelland & Stewart,
a division of Penguin Random House Canada Limited,
a Penguin Random House Company
www.penguinrandomhouse.ca

1 2 3 4 5   23 22 21 20 19

Penguin
Random House
McCLELLAND & STEWART

David and Sarah

CONTENTS

strange
attractor

Rain Self

Knotted coming and going, eider ducks rainwinged, blown off course, spent, after-storm crepuscular, a paddle's drip, scoop above half-buried cupboards of clams, saucers and spoons and cups without handles—scup, scoop—and on the surface, sleek face before birth, rippled, sliding. Face of an unknown self. Selfless, the same word backwards, selfless.

JAPANESE PRINT OF TWO FIGURES IN THE MOUNTAINS

Over the pass the messenger descends, through an early
snow squall. Tree sparkle, a whirl. Winter above,
another season below, and only one
diminutive figure on a trail. Even at a distance you know
what he's going to say. Your
son—

On the outcrops, those high shelves, snaggled pines are lifted, set
down in different places. Yet the mountain:
obdurate. You've prepared yourself,
but there's no containing it.
The man must be fed, given a place to sleep.
And the wind has picked up. It's autumn, so the leaves are dry,
curled at the edges. They shake their death rattle.

CROTON LEAF

A driver gauges the distance in the mirror, as the truck
begins its reverse, a processional, along the length of a white
driveway, brushing the saffron (not-quite orange, not-quite
crimson) maps on the dark green croton. Worlds within
what's known. Girlhood, a damselfly's whirring, underside
of a waxy leaf. Past condos and the wall around condos,
a barrier beach holds the tide at arm's length. Pushpull
of ocean, the unchanging law of gravity: nothing
that isn't normal. Turquoise, spread of darker ink beyond,
a cruise ship moored in airy wilderness, layered
taffeta, releasing slow poisons from its hull. Delivery,
pick up, the day's packages. The leaf blazes scarlet,
Pollock spattered with yellow-ochre; the truck backs up
as far as it can go into the loading zone. The beeping
stops. Now the soft clacks, the almost not heard palm clatter.

Someone raises her hands, shakes the branches. Tangents into grey air
with paper cuts of snow—a single Blackburnian warbler—above crystal
goblets hung in the trees. Tail-feathered winter, open river with slabbed
sides across low-slung Tantramar: can you hear the tinkling, the glassiness?
Foreign, the not-yet spring blur coming and going across the flats, and
that one lost bird, gilt-flecked.

(In a painting, a bird above hummocked earth, and within that painting
another marsh, freeze-shone, and the bird, repeated, smaller, and so on.)

Shimmered crucible. Orange slash, black edge, a bird come too early from
Columbia. The distance it has travelled: cinema, velvet half-thought. Heard,
now, as if hands have dropped snow strings along the aisles of the field. Salt
water stoppered by flap-gates of the aboiteaux—an ocean, held back. A bird released.

PARTY

Home in a home remade, nursing home lounge, crumpled mother,
father, scrolled cake, with balloons yours, mine, happy hovers,
scrolled rosettes cut into pieces, yours mine eighty-four, lick of
icing on a beard, plates and forks taken away, one daughter spreads
her napkin, another daughter dissolves, scene within an unnoticed
landscape behind Mona Lisa's shoulder where mother, father
might gaze from headlands, pinnacled rocks, loose elastic band
of beach

but no one walks into cloudspeech *Apatheia*

spacious

only a corridor with an empty gurney and two women wheeling
mother, father, heads sleep nodding, back to separate rooms.

CHEST OF DRAWERS

She'd already left to see her father's body for the last time. Late
March, a mother driving alone. Daughter

no longer daughter. At home,
the drawer hung open, slack
jaw.

He put his socks into the drawer, said her grandfather
had died

in the night. Socks unspooled from a father's hands,
dark tongues that told
a child
he'd died,
she'd gone,

but not in time. Abandoned,

the two of them, a younger father, younger daughter, crippled
by left and right, socks tucked

into the drawer.

Abandoned what was known
the two of them unspooled from a drawer
of fathers she'd already crippled those socks left and right he told
her he'd hung open slack told her she'd gone told her the dark tongue

knifed through died and dead. That he was not.
Not in the time they kept or any other. No tongue
no eye
no heart
no lung
no hand

no handle on the drawer. A clock still ticked,
sandwiches lay on plates in the kitchen, sliced
and ready to be eaten. What was left for them.

CUP

Seahorse hands, thwart and yank of a baby's body, swaddled cries, tick
and tick of a clock on a maple desk, glass gleamed bell, each minute
a vanishing trick. Is she sleeping? Here are books, photos, all the materials
needed for an experiment. Afternoon sun stripes a pillow, paper roofs
sag on a string across the living room. Wishes for a happy new year.
Outside, winter's upheaval.

Inside, light invents spoons in soup bowls, butter knives, toasted crumbs
on plates. Dorothy says anyone could spend hours looking, fingering
a silky nape, half-awake: she and John shared the night watch. Rebecca's
on the couch, cloudless sky in her arms. Stir honey into tea, sweet gold
unwound into slightly bitter, the day twisted and spooled and dropped into it.

OTHERWORLD

As if a door opened, as if you went through. Red dogwood alders,
~~frostfurred, bend~~
~~in~~ a path, autumn. ~~Stippled~~ distance, in the middle of—

No sound. Hear it, far-off, underside of cloud. Bend,
breath. Snow. Laddered wing of a heron, blurred, rising.

Lacework on a path. Souls brush air, brush ground.

Where to?

A language so unfolded it's almost gone.

So unfolded it's almost gone—a voice, not a voice, asking.

What ghosts this surface?

Otherworld,
otherworld.

Brushed distance, a door.

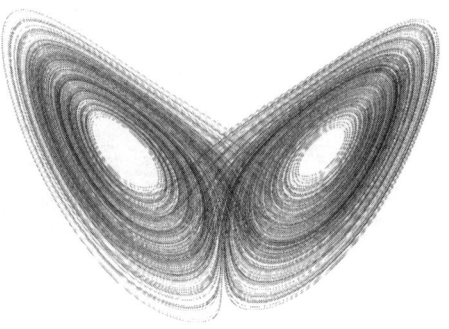

THE DRAWINGS OF SANTIAGO RAMÓN Y CAJAL

The Hippocampus

Inside the memory garden, pyramidal neurons. Clustered, dense. Spangled
hyacinths, purple florets thick on each stalk. Seen through scratched
panes of the French door with its elderly handle. She opens it, steps onto
white patio stones. Beginning of the world. Someone soothes a baby
on the other side of the hedge, a robin fusses in soil, trying to find what's lost.
Chill of stone under bare feet. Buckets of light pour and pour.

Glial Cells of the Cerebral Cortex of a Child

Her drawing of a pumpkin flutters in her hand as she runs
to her mother. Astrocytes pinwheeling in her brain, tiniest
of tumbleweeds, maybe already inviting the strangeness
inside.
See how she opens the door of the little house, laughing.
Too small for an adult, just right for a four-year-old. Secret
world. Bright hair falls across her face when the barrette
is loose. A red jacket

with a zipper that always catches. Flushed cheeks.
October.

The young woman smiles at the guests, disappears into the light-
striped corridor, manages to reach the kitchen. Champagne glasses
fall from the silver tray, almost out of hearing. Tumble, shatter.
Can she keep her balance long enough to sweep up the pieces?
Think of what just happened to the neurons in the spinal cord,
in the dorsal root ganglion. A wedding

party. They want the server to return with the drink order.
They clamour.

Her tray appears, levitating, rising out of golden-brown pond
water. Shimmer-bright cloud, not a tray. Here is a possible diagnosis:
open-backed speeches and pastel bouquets,

scented rose-pink, curl-lipped, evening. Someone beckons
from a linen-covered table, her pale arm. A delicate

message passes imperfectly to the brain.

SCAR TISSUE IN THE CEREBRAL CORTEX

We wander a yard sale of witchy trees. Forest of the unimaginable.
Someone speaks from a parallel world. She could be an oracle.
Here, an unlaced skate. No, a piece of Styrofoam. A radiant bottle

tilted, half-

submerged in the stream. She's not an oracle. She talks about contrast
dye, inflammation, lesions—what the MRI shows. Frozen archipelago
under water, a current slipped over ice islands. We try to catch up.
Birch, broken. Amputated elm. How long ago did we find ourselves
lost? East is pale lemon, streaked grey, spiked with spruce and more spruce.
Drugs aren't drugs, they're disease modification therapies. This is what
it looks like, but more will be known as we go along.

We nod.

She stops us at a threshold we thought we could pass through.
We watch a young woman

go on alone. Edge
of the woods, snowmelt, a single goose feather caught in curled grass.

She could be a tree leafed in yellow-gold, a ginkgo. She's waiting
for the neurologist to prescribe Tecfidera or maybe

Tysabri. Imagine axons, feather-threaded, unseen, passing gossip
along a party line. What does the story of the root have to do
with the story of the leaf? Underside, blindside.

She figured it out because of the optic neuritis.

Vibration, finger spark, on a finger-tipped trunk. Shiver tree.
The neurologist will tell her what she already knows.

Wrench
and
twist, wind. Bright-backed leaves, dance-skirted, turn inside out.

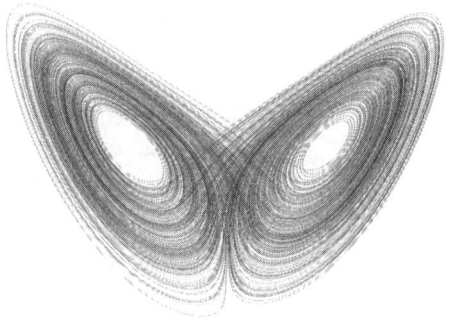

Courage is a Chair

The chair is always there. Whatever the story of your life,
the chair accepts your version of events.

You take your place, take the places of others who have been
and are not, take the place and have the place taken from you.

You might tell the truth, or not tell the truth and let it enter
your body as a lie that lives inside the truth, or the truth that lives
inside a lie, which could singe your skin and stop your heart
if you're buckled to the chair.

But this is a perversion of the chair's purpose.

The chair doesn't judge.

You might be sitting in a chair, almost asleep:
high chair, swing chair. Waiting for the spoon, the straw.
Waiting for the buzzer, the bell, the minute hand to form an alliance
with the hour hand. Waiting for the seat at the back, the seat at the front,
the seat no one wants. Waiting for the spoon, the straw.

The chair offers itself.
It bears your weight. It bears no weight.

It lifts you so you can look down from above. You'll see cities,
labyrinths of roads, cars moving on the roads,
and, in the distance, something flashing. A train.

What was so large that is now so small?

Black Tortoise of the North

Glass crosshatched with frost, and outside, Buddha
on the well. Bought at the Five to a Dollar, toupee of snow

askew on his head. Do the living resemble the dead
or is it the other way around? In the grocery store, my father

grasps a red-purple dome, Spanish onion, dissolves into someone
wearing a ball cap. I was wrong about winter. Buddha

gazes north, not east, nodding towards the cave of Xuan Wu,
mythical tortoise. Weight of cold on its back, a rope-thick snake

knotted around February. Under the willow, a woman holds up
her skirts. Her ankles, golden under water. She's no one

I know. A shore broken to bits, as if an axe had been thrust, thrown.
It rushes through, this dream, loaded shelves

of branches, dead loops of raspberry canes, hare's track
merely an unfinished sentence. My father's dead—

Half-closed eyes, cracks in ice. A last freight train winds uphill,
car after car. In the distance, singing, those souls without a home.

Change Room

Girls trying on dresses in the change room,
scattering clothes on the floor—maples and poplars,
honey locusts and oaks. You'd never know
these leaves were dying. Watch how they flit,
turn themselves inside out, slickered
yellow, orange, lipstick red. Adolescent
crushes: her promises, his sweet
talk, kisses behind the garage. It's true
they've given themselves over to what comes
next. Last things, yes, but first they're alight.
What we set out to be once, fearlessly. That fire.

As if through glass, light splinters. A choral concert,
not the funerals of February, March, for two boys who killed
themselves, one after

the other.

Voices swell into the Song of Solomon, winter
past, over and gone. Above the altar, a crucifix.

The arms of Jesus, hauled up
by his own fixed hands, body of stone. Domine ad adjuvandum
me festina.

I don't want to think about Jesus. It's April. It should be mild,

but quivers of arrows strike and fall, strike and fall against lancet
windows as the choir sings. Ice or sleet, percussion. Hanging

on a cross asphyxiates a human being. It'll be hell

driving home. Jordon, Scott. Ita filii excussorum.
They could have been in a choir, mouths making that perfect

O.

One tenor calls to another in the loft. Far-off reply. The face
of the crucified Jesus could be a boy's,
looking down

before he throws himself off

a rooftop in a small town. Flies into a blizzard, flecked
nightworld. Gloria Patri.

RED LEAF, YELLOW LEAF

What a child would pick up:

wet leaf faces, blotched by fat, black
tumours. Ruddy, red-tipped,
and yellowed.

Slick-sheen of all that's coming, pelt-
tongued. Rain and rain and rain

pooled, clotted on the grassy
path, narrow-
necked. Your friend, fresh
water and tidesurge, his diagnosis
slipped into weeds and willow roots, greasy-
spooned estuary. What we're told. Uncertainty, moon

tugged. Leaf stuck to a boot,
a brown-backed cut-out. Your friend
said thank you, holding on
to what the doctor gave him.

The size of it, the fact
of it. Scarlet leaf, yellow-orange
leaf. A child
with a pair of scissors can make
any kind of shape.

Stone Self

Once a man tried to get through the wall,
broke his femur. Now he gets signed in, signed out, signed in.

August in a square of window. A square for morning, for afternoon.

Whose face looks at him

in the bathroom? No one
knows him, not even his wife. He's given up

that self, cupboard of collectibles

rattler skin fish lures going to school in winter dark dark dark swinging
a lunchcan three conkers over the log at the stream a couple of broken
robin's eggs penknife with a fake mother-of-pearl handle pyramid
of beer bottles a girl downy feathers a raft a girl a raft fallen bottles
a river that time he got lost in the woods glass everywhere a wife
feathers children fake mother-of-pearl the name the name the name
of the one who comes to visit—

Self, still. Breath after breath.

Here's the nurse with a plastic container
of pills, glass of water. Where is he going? He swallows

round white stones, blind eyes.

GRACE

Finger the multiple clock hands of a silver
fan palm, the way it splays outward
as if to you, only you, even as it resists your touch.

Skin shrunk taut over the bone bed of what
was once a person. Thailand, a monastery, and here
in the House of the Dead, a scent of jasmine.

Sea fog. A freshly waxed convertible brakes on the pier,
rolls forward. A hammering, then a scrawl of laughter close by.
Why do we always want bread crumbs on a path?

She said the word grace, tilted her head just so.
Her glasses shimmered, could have held a vista of a Polish country house
in the nineteenth century, bridled horses being led out for walks.

She said the word grace, tilted her head just so.
Her glasses shimmered, could have held a vista of a Polish country house
in the nineteenth century, bridled horses being led out for walks.

Sea fog. A freshly waxed convertible brakes on the pier,
rolls forward. A hammering, then a scrawl of laughter close by.
Why do we always want bread crumbs on a path?

Skin shrunk taut over the bone bed of what
was once a person. Thailand, a monastery, and here
in the House of the Dead, a scent of jasmine.

Finger the multiple clock hands of a silver
fan palm, the way it splays outward
as if to you, only you, even as it resists your touch.

OTHERWORLD

Brushed distance, a voice

asking a question. Bole of a birch, hemlock, ~~fingertips of white.~~
~~Otherworld.~~

Dark water, silvered. Laden trees, wavering, ghost this surface. We crave pattern,
crave answers.

A bend, middle of a path, a toad. Questions slipped into evening's glove.

Snow, snow, snow.

Laddered underside of breath. Hear it—no sound.
Stippled cloud, stippled ground. Rising wingblur,

lacework

of dogwood alders, frostfurred souls,
imagined.

Autumn no longer autumn, but

brushed distance, a door into snow, snow, **snow.**

You opened it

WRESTLING

I stood
in front of a rope-handled door. Inside,
girls with slim hips, hands covering
breasts. They'd never known

a man. He said it was his right
(to see blossoms of blood seep into linen, darken).

He challenged me. Waited . . .

waited.

His eyes
hunted the soft, the slack. How could I fight him?
A king. Gilgamesh.

He threw me
against circling dogs. Dust. Salt on dry lips.

I flung him down. He lay
under cloud skiffs. Blue, rocking. Got up.

It went on, couldn't be won. Grappled each other's rock-hard body. Slippery,
two of us, slicked, one,
legs locked legs, arms linked. I panted into his ear. He

held on.

THE SPLIT

Self selved   here, doubled, blade-struck
split. I am Enkidu   but not Enkidu.

I'm neither wolf   nor man. What?
Licked my own foot once, a paw.   He licks my face without

touching.   He craves, king crowns.
Me.   What

do I want?   I ran beside the wounded
doe, staunched her   gored flank. I felt I was

I was I felt   her too. Racing
sweet tricked sweet stripped   me, wildering

bones thicketed. Smell this.   Ruddied, reddened. Deep self,
blood. I am Enkidu   who loves Gilgamesh.

FOREST

Who forbids us? No

one. But I'm afraid.
Inside fear is a knuckle-hard knot. Where I've never gone.

We're at the border, unseen line of trespass. Tangled alders, leaf
on leaf, ridged bark and root. Fretwork fern, coppery. Here

I'll lose myself.

I said I'd go with him, I wouldn't leave.

When he swings his axe, I'm not Enkidu. I'm the kerf he makes
in the trunk. Sway and crackling, thud, drawn-out deafening.

He said I made him feel like a god.

I'm myself and I'm not. Not the felled tree, only
the wound.

But you know this.

The Wound

Open the box of your life. The slat-step clatter

is the wound. I could say my arm, Enkidu's, was lanced
wrist to shoulder. I could say what happened—

It only matters to the story.

Gilgamesh killed Humbaba and saved me. You

saved yourself, child in a blind room. Moonless
middle of night, no bread crumbs. As if you were me. I, you.

Enkidu, fleet, foregone in tree shadow, pine needles crisscrossed on the ground,
printed golden-brown, sticky, on bare feet. You can escape

the story, not the wound.

To Enter the Door of That Forest

As if the trees knew how and what and when. In a day, a night,
how. A man, I

love a man. Here on the moss, I rode him. Let me say it, no—

Shout.

Did you hear

our slapped skin? Throat-guttered kiss, gush, brine. One body
between us. Cradled in him, him in me, warmth. As if
an oil lamp, shell-shaped, size of a child's palm. Glow
spun. I go

after him

into the shudder. He could twist a dagger into me, the one
engraved with a lion. I'd let him. He pauses to touch my neck,
lipped nape, stroked tender, stroked. King slaved
to what he wants. Under my tongue, honey.

At the back of his knees, salt. Torqued

taste, othered. But

                                        I shouldn't have come into it.

            Now Ishtar nightmares herself inside him, sends Heaven's Bull.

He yelps, wakes. I hold him with one arm; the other arm useless, swollen. Pain
    has a century's length. The forest presses close, spear-branched. It did this

                                        to me. Bait with baiting
whisper men, these trees, each trunk a cudgel, hooded glances of the leaves, turned.

Into the Sound Of

I tell him to go on without me, but
he can't. We lie

together, catch

fingered. Stream's up-bubbled swirl. Mostly we don't
speak. I want him

to tell me of the box kite, where it went, boyhood. Torn

length, bloodied, of the arm he bound, mine. Wanting to live
as if I were him. Across the stream, dusk, its mosses, the deer's flag,
jounced rump with a white snap. How I could speak that

morning grey. His

voice,
wove-soft fog. Stones, I'm not
walking now, each
footstone. Thirst. Dying
begins outermost, then
seeps. Fingertips,
whorled. Come-apart
self. Moaned. To drink
the both-place dream before
it goes.

WATERSKIN

From him, into the slipped halfway, almost ready, I am

just a white stone toothed under waterskin. Groan-caught, gripped,

yes, but pain smalls it. Largeness I gave, unlimit, unbound,

Gilgamesh

dressed in your own wail. I hear it. Wound

seared, my not-yet scar to be buried in. Agony, steeped

stink. Do this. Let me—you see, gone from gleaming, I am

my death, I make it

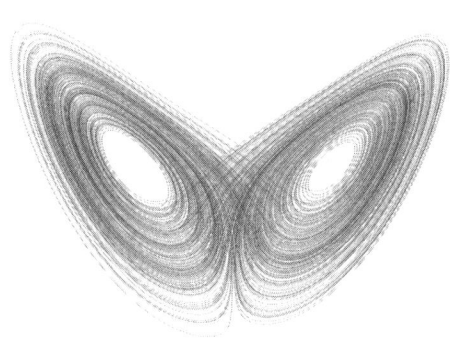

SPELL

Sleep skin, almost breath. Such private
eyelids, swaddled.

Here, dream.

Come, proud, with shook manes, rope-
taut sheening. Sweat horsed.
Be bridled, be hitched, large
bodied and stamping. Up

and gone,
smoke
on moonglass. Night flint. Quick the hooves, quick

the breath. Home

whistled, currycombed,
full fed and sweet talked. Now

traveller, open.
Eyes, morning tipped.

Grass Self

A man dozes in a chair on the deck. Poplar chatter of silver-green,

silver-white, silver-green.

How he's gone away, come back.
At night, when she opens the cupboard of his chest,

she finds herself
long-limbed, smooth-skinned, many selves

ago. Branching poplar, shivered air. Shivered water. Cormorant
after cormorant skimming air, water, air. Time,
what it wants.

Stones, clocks. The slick
of what remains in the bottom of a glass on a table.

How they didn't care. How they lay with their legs outstretched.
Spokes on the grass.

In Burlington

"Oh hell, here's that dark wood again" —KIM ADDONIZIO

Middle of nightwood, a suburb. A springy Labradoodle tries
to leap the fence, scenting coyotes, or maybe coywolves,
in a driveway. Topaz-glimmered gaze, nothing like a dream,
exhaled breath in cartoon balloons, frost-crisp. The dog
throws itself against the gate, can't shut up. Acid, pale yellow,
eats the moon. Monster homes straddle a ravine, greasy streak
of water down its navel. In garages, Subarus click and flare
and cheep goodnight. Listen for the clack of heels, a woman
who took the 6:43 from Union Station, oblivious to all
but Brandon—such an asshole, a *real* asshole—on her cell,
as infinite realms open above the hemlocks and white pines,
bitch-slapped by wind, each branch a knotted length of rope.
A corner Cape Cod with a tidy living room; flickered glimpses
of golfers on a green. Someone's going to strangle it—that *dog!*

Lightning Self

Man in the mirror not looking in the mirror, lightning
in his chest. Clang
of no self within the self. No time to call out to his wife,
no word

to give it a name before he's

underwater, a sunken boat. His arms open, his ribs, open.

Judge of the clam beds, judge of the tidal inbreath, outbreath, judge
of the eelgrass, thickening in the shallows.

Clear water, utterly clear. Speechless.

The white stones ask:
Who are you?

The black stones ask:
What have you done?

The grey stones murmur, murmur.

Cool slippage, draw and slide. Windless evening, ladle and turn
of the paddle. Over Sugarloaf, the golden chalices, spilled.

Field of hay, field of barley.

Cake without Bride and Groom

AFTER *(cake) forest (hubert)*, MIXED MEDIA, 2007, BY FIONA KINSELLA

That silver,
can you hear it? A nuthatch rests
in your hair, flits off. Leaves unwind and unwind
in the rattling turn of a helix. Almost dawn. Let's not
go back to where we said we'd be. Papery rustle, squirrel
on a branch. Let's find the place where hemlocks
lean against night. Someone snipped the moon
out of the sky, sent it
rolling. Catch it, love,
you who are helpless with laughter.

First Sutra

Late winter, a dog under the white pine
tries to get up.

Sheen of ice near the shore. Farther out
it's all breakage. An estuary full of silver bowls, silver

hammers. Bowls beaten by hammers.

Tries, fails. He gets up,
pisses, takes a step, pisses.

Collapses on pine needles, stitched snow.

Ears the colour of caramel, familiar
velvet. Already a ghost in his body. Eyes

darkened.
Entered and gone into. Paragate.

Two steps forward, hind legs crumple.
Time to call the vet.

Water, moving.
No sound, only the glint of the hammer, turn of the bowl.

Parasamgate.

Blood on the paw. Point
of stoppage: eyes, heart. Breath

no breath.

Body of a dog,
heavy in the flower-patterned sheet
folded double to carry the weight.

I see her in yellow, not Vermeer blue. The merest hint
that she's pregnant, the young woman reading the letter
in the painting. Roasted vegetables, rosemary. Withheld
taste of cashew. Cindy says she's never paid attention
to Dutch art. But which part of the letter trips her up?
Charlie interrupts, wants to know about the landscape
framed above the fireplace. Hurt, so small, tucked in.
We turn to face it, cloudy shreds over black mountains,
probably a driving rain somewhere. Plates pushed back,
napkins crumpled. Cake tipsy on its pedestal. One or two
of the men are drinking amber from doll-sized glasses.
Maybe he's not coming back now the war's over, or
he's taking the long way home. She folds the letter,
slips it in her bodice. That aftertaste, it could be honey.

closed it, opened
another door. Frostfurred, wintered. Whoever leaves, returns
with hands of cloud. Undone.

~~Any face holds~~ another face, the one before
birth.
~~Rippled, lucent,~~
a current under ice. Who speaks of endings?

Undone.

Pins flung against glass, snow translated to ice translated to rain.
Passages of light, grey-hemmed.

~~Spun, spinning—ecstasy~~
~~of whirl. Pulled underside of cloud, spiralled white. Storm~~
turn of a dervish,

otherworlded world.
Who speaks of endings speaks beginnings.

(43)

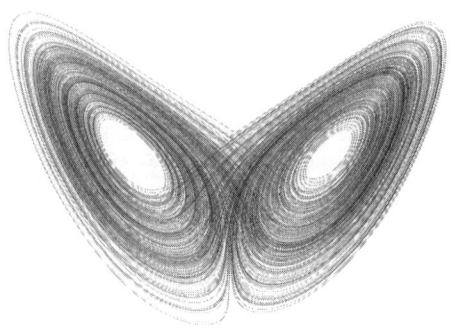

STRANGE ATTRACTOR

Let's say your life makes a shape

that doubles what's already there. Another life, also yours,
but unseen. Give it a kitchen,

some cups on a shelf, dishes patterned with blue fish,
a garden, maybe some poppies with coral taffeta skirts. A canvas-backed folding
    chair
by the door, binoculars. A borrowed beach
house.

Go outside, look

from this vantage point. Ocean, a cloth
slid across a table. A blurred barge, a tugboat.

It comes into focus,
but there's also transparency. A brush dipped in blue, almost purple, still blue,
drawn along a gauzy scrim, so the upper edge is rucked, uneven:
a gesture called mountains. It'll never overwhelm

your real life, the one that takes you
to the laundromat. These are separate, finite-dimensional systems.
You sit by the washing machine, listening to the spin cycle. The evolving

variable can be represented algebraically. Thirty years ago,
you painted a picture of a hollyhock by the same house, same beach. It floated
    away, discarded.

That hollyhock,

that life

represented algebraically as an n-dimensional vector: you can't
see it no matter how hard you try. Come out of the laundromat.

It's noisy and you're tired. Too many coins fed into the machine,

one thing after another to be folded. Soft sheets, mended,
several beige towels.

A hidden life, this other one. Elusive, though you've given it a sofa
with a Peruvian blanket, a large window, a door that opens.

Tangled fragrances: salt, sweet. Ruby aril of the yew.

The yew, the Douglas fir, the hemlocks, the sword
ferns turning brown at the tips. And here,
a smaller scale. The underside

of the foxglove leaf. Candelabra branches over velvet

green. And a spire of creamy blossoms, puckered,
not yet open, that can stop
or heal the heart. Two sides of the same thing. Go into the kitchen,

sit at a table drinking coffee as if
you're drinking coffee, thirty years cupped within thirty years. The strange

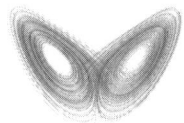

attractor can be a region in *n*-dimensional space. Back then, Margo
took pictures

of the irises in a shallow blue bowl. A wedding. People arrived in pairs,
in clusters across the lawn, women's heels sinking into grass. Rain
had come and gone, silver-white

stitched lace, a passing thought. Chiaroscuro.
Sun, shadow, sun, satin. If a vow is spoken does it hold its shape?

Something is about to burst, buttery yellow. Downy
foxglove petals are marked with hieroglyphs, each a miniature door
to be opened.

One: Silking the firs, Hunter's moon snow.
Two: Burning—a miniature Japanese teahouse—shōji screens ablaze.
Three: Nothing can be read into
a language no one can translate.

The sound of your days is a finger around the rim of a glass. You hear
a man dying.

He once told you
your own father had vanished

into music. A nest by the kitchen door. If the evolving variable—

You make another

nest beside the one at the top of the wooden shutter,
hidden. Perfectly rounded, made to fit,

though he's gone, your father. Nothing but ghost twigs, woven
with down.

Anyway, it's invisible,
unlike the one you see each time you go in and out. High,
but not out of reach. You speak quietly to the man who is dying.

You say rest. Rest
here.

You could say all that he's given, it's enough,
but he's sleeping. He's between.

A boat passes Savary Island towards Hernando and Mitlenatch,
a southwest wind, white sails the colour of water: it could be

hovering

as it completes a circle in air, but it moves out of sight,
up the Strait of Georgia. If the evolving
variable is two- or three-dimensional

then the attractor of the dynamic process can also be represented
in the multiple dimensions of
dawn,
dusk,
dawn,
dusk, as if
it mattered. Yet it matters. Faint
ringing on the rim of a glass. The slightest

tilt leeward, suck and smack of lapping.

Ocean,

ocean.

He wavers. His wife is steady,
leaning over him to listen.

How it goes apart and stays together. How the words
make and unmake themselves. See,

here's the bed that held you, night boat. Smooth
the sheets, thump the pillows. Last night, you lay awake for hours,
passed through door after door. A few Dutch phrases

spidered a page, the lamp's cone elongated into a straw hat,
a bonnet, and beyond the yellow light, the straight-legged
table, chair. Dream

table, dream chair

standing where the world thins. You went backwards

to pick up the story. Babies in their bassinets, the sound of each
one alone, not alone. Morning babble, milk. A spoon

flung on linoleum. Laughter: a straw hat, then a bonnet. Silly
spoon, lying bowl-side up.

Thirty years you've slept, woken,
slept. Before drifting off, you put

your hand on his chest, warm

skin. The orbits of two people, going away from each other, returning
not the same, but

the same. Married to the underside of the foxglove leaf, soft
nap, wild at the verge. Belled, not belled, Babylon tower

of purple. The black-tailed deer appear,

pause

for the human noise, warp wail. Once some sequences have entered

the attractor, nearby points diverge. A truck rounds
the bend. Skewed from a half-opened window, a half-elbow
of song. *Lost*—

Leap of doe, leap of fawn, straggling afterthought
of swallowtail. Dust follows.

Nearby points diverge from one another without departing
the attractor. Out of nothing,

two people, a couple of deer, a foxglove in a ditch, many
languages of purple, and an orbit of grit, yellow-gold at this hour,

settles,
settles on the road.

You're in the middle of it, breathing.

You're in the middle of it, breathing.

Your hand on his chest, warm—
Leaning over him to listen. Here

a language no one can translate. Thirty years cupped

within thirty years. The strange

tangled fragrances: salt, sweet. Ruby aril of the yew,
discarded.

Go outside, look.

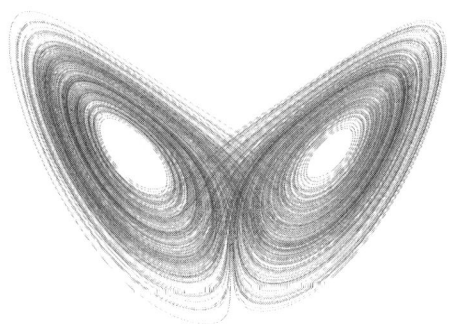

HERACLITUS

If you step into this stream now
and return an hour later, everything
will be different. Step into this tea-
steeped water, with a few strands
of grass turned September Blonde.
Between the person you are
to the person you will be after
you step out of this stream,
after you've wiped your eyes,
after you've had one child, then two,
then maybe three, or none at all,
you'll look up and find yourself
studying the grand theories
of clouds, one construed as
a woman with her arms outstretched,
another as a burning house. If you
step into this stream, the one
outside the library, not very deep,
with a shopping cart rusting
on its side, you'll feel it around
your ankles. Step into the stream
when you're fifteen, lose one
of your running shoes (a red
one), and climb up the bank, damp,
shivering, and you'll be sixty-three.
Go back down to the stream
to get the shoe and you'll be
thirty-seven. If you step into this
stream now. If you step into
this stream if you step
if you return if you step. If you
return an hour later you can wrap
dusk around your shoulders. You
might hear someone tinkering

with piano keys, trying to plink
a tune. Let yourself be stream, let
yourself be where it comes from and
where it's going, let yourself be
nothing but a smear of traffic lights,
glossed ruby, glossed green, on the surface.

SECOND SUTRA

Her husband is with her at the concert.

> One man on the violin,
> the other on the piano. Franck's Sonata in A Major,
> finished for his friend on the day of his wedding.

After the concert, he takes her arm,
helps her down the steps.

She turns back, smiling, as if to apologize
for blindness in one eye, detached
retina.

> Cherry trees, halo of blooms.
> The groom plays a sonata for his bride.

> When he is old, he plays it
> from memory. The audience can hardly see the violinist,
> only his bow, and sometimes the shine
> of his violin. They hear the darkness only

when it's over. Ten days later,
her husband will collapse on the bathroom floor. Now

> the violinist snaps the clasps on his case.

Quick heels on pavement, car doors opening
and closing. Crows, invisible
in the soft pines near the cathedral, tin cup
of moon on a hook.

Rowboat

Oars in oarlocks, hauled through water, feathered over water.
Desolate, repeated.

She's the colour

of ocean. She's glass. A rower looks back to where she's come
from, not ahead.

She didn't set out to kill herself.

To row in a circle, one arm does most of the work, while the other
arm makes light strokes or no strokes.

She didn't set out to kill herself and then she did. She set out.

Helpan, häjlp, helfa. Help. If the mind is full of knife flight,
tern skitter, how can anyone
be heard?

How her son—

So close to the shore. This is where the danger lies.

Her son swam hard, almost tipped the rowboat getting into it.
She was still alive.

The rowboat is white, with a blue stripe. Its oars are varnished.

But there was never a rowboat.

There was a woman, a son. When he found her she was still alive.

The sound of oars in the oarlocks, then nothing
except terns. Plunk and sloop of water against the boat's hull.

IMPOSSIBLE STAIRCASE

AFTER *Relativity*, LITHOGRAPH, 1953, BY M.C. ESCHER

The man with a sack over his shoulder
could be going upstairs to bed
or down to a kitchen to tumble carrots on a board.

That drumming—I can't

fathom it. Tell me what you're certain of. Stay

like that, let me put my head on your shoulder. I'm tired
of the slideshow. Slick fabric of a down jacket, throb

of sinuses. The man on the staircase
has no face. Green sky, clouds puffed into eclairs.

At the top of another staircase, a couple, arms
around each other's waists. He's had a stroke; she's had cancer.
Such tenderness in the way he speaks to her. A pear tree

beyond them. You can see that,
can't you?

I'm not dreaming?

DELTA

Fizzed,
green cool
Puntledge swelled
by Courtenay, rivered
into grey slack, slubbed on,
slathered through, creeked
and braided, as if by hand, fresh
into salt, loosely woven. Flat, flat, flat.
Trick gulls, stuck heron. One toy plane
drills air. Benches with brass plates, for John,
for Wilma, for the Evergreen Seniors Chorus.
Asphalt path, boy on a bike. Maple leaf crumple,
devil's club, dry grass. Simmer. Mid-afternoon siesta
of streamwork across sand, sucked this way, that way,
arthritic fingers rucking the blanket below the half-blind
windows of condos. Unknown, the Kurile Islanders, landing
and leaving, mere water script, thousands of years old. Colder sea,
kelped theatres under the current. How a man lay in the canoe's hull,
sensed a wave pattern, a wind change. Wayfinding with stars or without,
as if islands were sparks inside his skull. Grey sand slips over this, disguising
the history of who was here when, arrivals and departures, so their lives cross,
tangled into those of the K'ómoks and Pentlatch, and those who took, Spanish,
British, and those who came later, Chinese, Japanese, German, Vietnamese, Syrian,
fresh into salt, salt into fresh, muscled wash and buckle, the long, long, roll call of tide.

Oak

Unvarying light in a robin's-egg room. Outside, men laughing.

Chain saws again.

Yesterday, racing that strip of sedges and sweet
grass and rolled-up red parasols
of sumac between the six-lane expressway and a railway:

two deer. The rattling

vertebrae, a freight train, headed towards Toronto, nowhere.

Homelessness,

rain. A burlap-shouldered owl, stricken

on a branch in the attitude of a sage or a convict.

Now the chain saw stops. Air
thrums. The furniture in every room

of my body upended, as if

after a burglary. Shudders, explodes crackling.
It goes

down, clouts ground. Neighbours' houses
shake. One
hundred
two hundred
two hundred and fifty years.

CLOUDBOAT

An orchard that's abandoned any idea of orchard. Here, three women,
blue footcaves of their tracks. Snāw, Old English. Sneo
or snjór.

Snihyati
from Sanskrit. You could say storm-lost, but it's only a slope they wade,
all

gradual.

Trucks muffled on the highway, drone of gears. Cladded. Gone wild,
wildered, each mottled apple with its cap, feathered millinery.

Slow-bodied women, year added to year as they step
lift
step
lift.

Schnee, heaps of dirty laundry by the road. A distant

plow scrapes past. Luxury of woolly-topped handrail, boots sunk
down and down to the unseen footbridge, made of toothpicks.

No crossing to the far snaygis,

pillowed śnieg. Where is the ferryman, the boat of cloud?

Trees bow for selfies of laden
branches in mirrorwater. Cuts through the heavy-sweet, this black brook

cleaving with its blade
a long oblivion, a dream of white and white and white. The extravagance.

OTHERWORLD

Hear it

against glass. Rain, its hundred thousand words. You're
translated—

Wavefroth tumbled in and in and in.

Springsurge and ebb. Out and out and out.
Foam's lacelapped hem on sand.

Othervoice. This
dervished water, spun skirt. Traced
joy, so unfolded it's almost gone.

Surge and ebb.

Speech of sea fronds,
Speech of water over sea fronds.

Unnamed trace. Glovepull of the vernal turn, a moon
so tender, unnamed. Unvoiced
O.

Only this,
how gone you are.

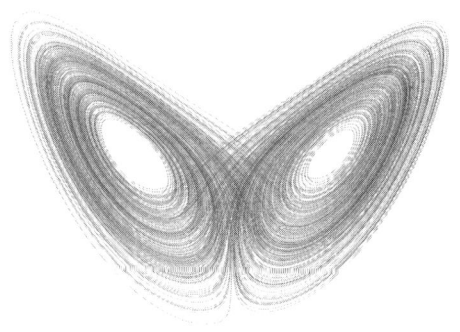

I CAN'T TAKE YOU

WHAT AM I NOW?

You've gone, Enkidu. Time won't have anything to do with you.

You wanted me to drag your body to the creek bed, water loose-streamed
over skin, bones.

Caterwaul in the alder weave, some injured raven. No, closer, clawing
up my throat, feather-tucked bird black.
What am I now?

In time out of time. Shiver, O, left me here, yowling through wing-bitten
craw. You, rigid on my lap.

The dead have no say. But how can I nest you in alders for birds to pick,
pock, pick? Lop-eared coyotes, maybe a wolf. They'll feed
on you as I do. Thinking

is ravenous. I slide you off my lap, stand. Night-swooned
king of surpassing

nothing. No one will know how love turns, snaps,

bites air. It's cold. I have no spade to dig a hole; the ground won't give.
How could I cover you? Me, you—pieces. One foot, the other,
neck, arms, collarbone,
chest span, that bridge
our eyes
made, skin smell,
faint
mint and lemon, that

taste. I can't take you. I can't.

Leave

Even if I didn't want to carry you, I'll wear leaving
as iridescence, hard shell of shimmering. Abalone. You inside me.

I have a question

for you. It goes out, it curves; I follow it.

WINTER

. . . .
. . . .
. . . .
. . . .
. . . .
. . . .
. . . .
. . . .
. . . .

Where did you go?

By a freeze-bright river, I hunch over a coyote's raw heart, liver.
My smeared mouth. Here, under cauled trees, white basketed
fingerbones of ice.

Am I you?

Snow, snow, snow. Red flourishes traced in a drift, unknown
language. From my own hands, blood. Or I could be in a room
filling up with whiteness. No river, no coyote.

Are you me? O—

I'm torn open. Snow, snow, snow,
snow, snow, snow, snow.

Do you hear it? The faraway
falling.

. . . .
. . . .
. . . .
. . . .
. . . .
. . . .
. . . .
. . . .
. . . .

The Hut

At night when I lie down, flashing

lions, mountains. I travel that roaring to the sun's end, dapple
garden. Evening, my brain picnics on stories. I tell myself it's a quest.

It's not a quest. It's grief. It has landscapes. Water, an island, a hut.

Haven't you opened the door of the hut hundreds of times, wanting

to know? There's no answer. I found the flower, nearly crushed it.
Honey on its petals, clustered together in a bee-sized dome. I could say

I did it for you, Enkidu. I tried

to bring you back.
Dream bloom, your face. I lost you. I woke afraid.

WHERE YOU ARE NOW

Maybe you're the hut and I'm the door. Not even a table
when I go inside.

Let's say the netherworld is the middle of the night when
I can't stop myself going into the hut. I burn it.

I set myself on fire burning it. Fire, then cold water.

I'm still here.

There's no end to you.

Thigh-soft night sloped behind trees. Hoot
owl. If I wait
long enough, I'll catch a glimpse.

In the Tedium

I go into days and nights, one after the other. A cup set down,
a scraped chair.

Outside, a coyote, tangled yelps. Moon, the way it lies

on snow. Snakebite blue.

I get up, stone.
I sit down, stone. King of morning, noon, night. Eat each stone,
spit it out.

This is what's called normal.
It isn't normal. It's deathwater.

Don't let me lose the sound of you. I'll make a raft of your laughter.
My nose against your nose. Your tongue—
O, now it's stone.

What have I done to you?

HOME

Afterwards, I open my eyes to the rushing.

As if I've been sick for years.

Someone has brought me a bowl. I bring a miracle
to my lips, drink it. Clamour, city of voices. Hearing the firmness
of the table,

the striped light. The three-legged stool is on the verge

of telling a joke.

I was never a king.

Enkidu, be gentle with me. I'm so small. A heavy-headed blossom
with a hundred pink tipped ears. It can't be found this time of year.
Ordinary. Not much scent, but a taste,

something I knew as a child.

Box kite, running, a hill. Clover on the hill.
How I fell down, laughing.

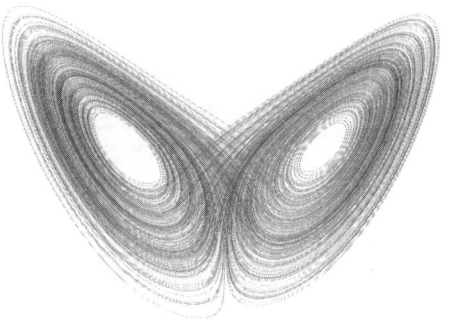

Mangrove, pewter-coloured ocean. Power lines. Nothing
to remind me of a verdant lawn, your hands speckled, maybe
flecked with brown sugar, tugging a low branch to show
its secret. Here they cycle past—one, two, three, four—
then a teenager slithers on a skateboard. I was eleven; you
were sick, not knowing what had seeded in your lungs. Below,
prisoned in the tangle, a boat (bloated life-vests, single oar)
half-full of water. A stuffed and knotted plastic bag hangs
from bones. Elbows, ankles, spines. Anything but this mess
of mangrove, its throng and thrust, slangy imperative. Don't
we want the great trees of the Botanical Gardens instead?
Heavily laden mahogany, black olive, banyan, kapok, acacia,
tamarind: each one named and numbered. But no
monkey puzzle, impossible to climb. Not this, not you.

GREEN SHINE

All this is new: bougainvillea, the almond trees'
reddened leaves, each one a parasail blooming
in air that is not air, more like a veil over skin.

Roosters jerkily step in circles, relentless
in their woodling. Such opera stars.

Nothing's new. Years pouring into years pouring
into years. We were here once, dirt-tired, grit
under our eyelids. These half-forgotten

roosters, green shine of plumes, showy droop. The peck,
peck, peck. Planes still take off, land,
full of those who come to occupy
the territory. Now I can hardly make out

your face, how you squinted against a sheet of foil—
water, sun—rumpled corner of the tent between your fingers

before we bent to set it up. Let me say beloved
because there's not much time. We hadn't lost
a parent then, no sister had cancer. Hadn't lost a child

that was never a child. That blue, maybe
cerulean or turquoise. We weren't used to the heat, tidy packages
of houses, white streaks tailing out behind the boats. Egret feathers.

MOON SELF

Making holes in daylight's about-to-be, childhood's room
squashed into toadstools,
someone with a saw. How to pass through?

A bowl of raspberry punch tips onto a bed in her parents' house.
Wolf moon, snow moon, seed moon: a woman half-awake.
Give it an hour. Half-frozen, axe-split

moon and sun in the same sky, doubled face. Spills over,

this month of bowls.
A woman who'd like to live elsewhere sprawls on a bed
in her parents' house. A chain saw in her brain, making holes

in ice. She can't get up, doesn't want to put her feet on the floor.

Nothing

moves. No fishermen yet, charcoal marks
on white.

Crooked in willow, an eagle. Below, small animals, curled
and sleeping. This month,
what shape

will it take? Wolf moon, snow moon, seed moon. In daylight's
about-to-be, a woman in childhood's room. Call it depression.
A bowl of raspberry punch

tips onto the bed. An hour or so,

and they'll be eeling on the ice. A couple of snowmobiles,
aluminum cans squashed into toadstools, someone making
one hole, another.

THIRD SUTRA

                                    Cut-paper blue, a slope, single tree,

plaid slippers on a tiled floor. A man
with a broken femur gets up, slides
a walker on tennis balls past the nursing station.

                              On the branches of the elm, party hats,
                                              doll-sized. Shaken

                                        in a northwest wind,
                                              shivered toss

of thoughts. She hasn't
visited for a week. No, eight
days. Can't be

right. Now she's here,
her walker's folded in the solarium.
Aluminum containers have been set out,
each cardboard lid tilted. The ginger beef
has leaked on the fake wood, sticky
pool. He floats,

door to table. Balances on one foot—

                                              Dancer.

Should he kiss her?

It's true that women look older in the afternoon light
than men of the same age. As for the small rugs
of the elbows, we could regard them as jovial. Let's
move forward. Discuss late Gothic style in the paintings
of the Très riches heures du Duc de Berry. You wish
you could hear it, the draftsmanship of morning,
the way precision lends itself to trees. Did you see a fox
between the alders? The calligraphy of its tracks, frozen
until spring. By then we'll be in pieces: so much ice gliding
over the globe. Inner becomes outer, a cape lined with white
silk. Your inconsequential fevers pulled inside out, amygdala
with its folding maps of world history. Size of an almond.
Go back to infancy as cloud. Hey where r u? Cirrus,
cumulonimbus. We've never stopped talking to ourselves.

CICERO

Dead pines, sparse broom bundles on branches. Widowed
landscape after the Battle of Philippi. Study in brown, this

grove, amber glints of October, and the dog's quest, circling
a scent in the clearing. Caesar's murder put Cicero on the wrong

side of history. Aftermath of wrangling, civil war. But how to stop
a tyrant? Moss proliferates without roots, anchors. A plume

of red-gold across these tufts. My friend's boy wants to be free,
and still bind himself to what he loves. A calfskin page: non nobis

solum. Cicero's invocation to his son. Be critical of a leader
who allows the people no rights. Follow nature, follow wisdom.

Sphagnum, peat, goldthread. Peppery bayberry. Maybe we're larger,
maybe less. He knew they would come. Once larvae are in the bark,

white pine weevils ravage trees for miles around. Any scavenger
wants a feed. When Cicero was caught, they cut off his head

and hands; his tongue was a gift to Fulvia. Mouth without words.
Non nobis solum. We're not born for ourselves alone, but for those

we don't know. Jewel-green moss spreads and spreads, unnoticed
eloquence. We take the path uphill as the wet-nosed dog careens.

DEADLIFT

Wide stance, arms locked. Deep breath, grip the bar, take it
from the floor, heavy plates on both sides. You know the story,
you don't know it. Lift it above your knees, higher, the enormity
of that weight. Hold the woman you don't know, hold
her son's distance—blue hyphens of water glimpsed
in passing—hold the man telling the woman about another
woman. She doesn't want to hear. Turned sails of the poplars,
teenager at the side of the road tying his shoe, six or seven
junked cars in a row, open-mouthed. The woman who knows
the man won't make her any promises. Her anger. A flare
of wild roses, butter-and-eggs, a few beer cans crushed, ditched:
and the complex arrangement of the white-throated sparrow's sweet
Canada, Canada, Canada. Lock it in, haunt and piercing. Let it go.

OTHERWORLD

How far

you've travelled. Beyond wintermelt, sprung light, into
air. Absence, presence, absence.

Gusted across water.
Wind to ocean, ocean to wind, wind to ocean.

Afterwards,
still,
still,
still.

Glassy surface,
unnamed traces in a glassy surface. In and in and in.

As if a door opened,
as if you went through.

Cloudy underside of breath. Hear it.
no sound.

A door, opened. How unreturned
you are, and yet——

Bent passages of light, grey-hemmed. blurred, as if
you were a word
in the language of rain.

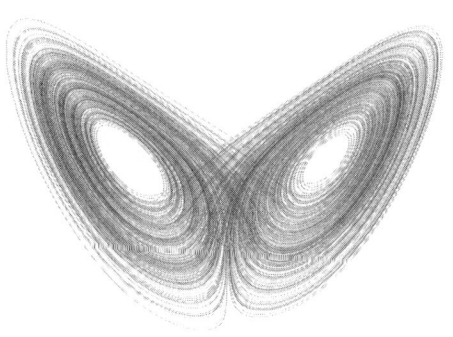

TEST

What season is it?

Upside down on branches, umbrellas. Smears of chartreuse, birches and maples.
Pin cherries, about to whiten. Thrust,
season of what can't be heard, but

touched, as if we were blind until
the not-yet lilacs in the neighbour's garden. Noses, tight buds.

Poodle in a backyard, barking. And two girls, one with a shiny can to her ear,
the other with a can
to her mouth, a string between. Me, you.
Talker
listener
gaggler
giggler. Look, behind:

running down glass. I know there's a question in it. One
beaded slipper, then another, and then
so many you can't tell them apart. Years. Outside, blurred
chapels of trees.

Backwards into poodle,
string to mouth, shiny
can to barking,
ear to girls,
two
between lilacs, listeners.

That season.

Where are you?

I was a child; it was morning. Hanging on the screen door,
a Luna moth. Wing

silk, earlobe-soft. Purple-trimmed, marked
with eyes. Moth with no mouth, eating nothing for a week. Mating,
dying, like the one clinging to a mesh of wire. Pale green.

You're asking me questions to see—

When I rub the brown islands on the back of my hand, the ridged veins,
you think I don't understand.

The moth could have come from another world.

                              Where?

We can live in more than one place
at a time. I'm here

in this room, beside you. It's darker than you think
and the air is one velvet dress after another I am less than

the size of my two hands, side by side, fingers outstretched,
translucent, almost.

There are three objects on the desk. I'll name them.
Now you name them.

You name each thing, set it down
where it levitates,
shivers in the topaz gleam across your desk. Three in a row, eldest
to youngest.

This and this and this.

My turn.

The piano lid bangs shut. I'm only eight, I want to say, but we both know
I've slipped into starlings
shaken loose from the Norway maple when the piano lid slammed,
scattershot, the hundredfold
wings gathering into soar, how soar can be under and over
itself, a knot
that doesn't loosen into this,
and this,
and this.

Add by sevens.

Seven, the shape of someone who turns around, body canted against a trail's slope. Seven plus seven is fourteen. Fourteen plus seven. I am more and less than. Struck, stricken. Gaze cluttered by frayed prayer flags of the poplar. Beyond, sand fingerings in far blue-grey, each barrier beach an upturned palm washed, washed, washed. What's coming, tide-dragged seals, days and months. Corpses, slick-backed, stinking. Twenty-one. I see the vista. Easier to think of these crows filching through birches, whup, whup, whup. Once I was thirty-five, but who was she? Thirty-five plus seven, plus seven, plus seven. A woman stands at the hinge where her life opens. Here I am made to step into water, air. Too old to go forward, too young to go back.

We talked about these three things on the desk.
Can you name them?

Each thing is empty. It waits
to be filled. Let me sing to my hands, folded. I have work
to do, never enough hours. Maybe I was a mermaid
who became a human. A mistake,
said the witch who took my tongue. Lost

is curled inside found, flight
a riddle of bone and feathers. I am most myself
when I'm not.

Three things.

A hat brim, Venus, a cup.

Or
love, a handle, one brown goat.

Or
scissors, forgiveness, a mottled leaf beaded with seed pearls.

Barn

As if it were a skull, exposing Broca's area, Wernicke's,
that trembling

glimmer between them. Spacious emptiness, forked
thoughts in and out. Hayloft gloom, unwanted
hay

floats across boards, wobbled light, morning

in the gaps above. A myth, what swallows took
from sleeping gods, how it burned

their tails. Soon no one will know

anything nested here, in cups of mud, grass. They'll take it down
to feathered

nothing. The singed
tail streamers, shape of

what was
and is not. They'll take down this barn.

A brain with neural loops unseen, the passages of blue-

hooded birds holding it in place.

MAN, FALLEN

A man throws out his arms, topples on cut crystal. He crawls, can't
make sense of his knees. Gazes into a crack, edge of shiny wrapper,
milk foam and grit, hundred-billion-year-old glints in a black, black realm.

He tries, tries again. A woman parks her Silverado, one wheel high on a snow
bank, slams the door and helps him up. Holds him as if they're newly married.
It's gone, whatever he saw, galaxy on galaxy, opening one into the other, even
the farthest nebulae, stung-bright. Her step, his step, a sort of waltz on an icy
sidewalk. Shiny wrapper, foam, grit, the hundred-billion-year-old sparkles
in the black, blacker realm to which they once belonged.

Taming the Bull

The whole thing had been a dare. The first fierce days were spent warily,
one skirting the other. The man forgot he'd come to tame it. In the evening,
lying on the bank, he smelled what he couldn't name. Was it wolf willow?
He'd come into the meadow to throw a rope around its neck. Now
when he slept, he saw the creature's curved horns. Legs not sickle-hocked,
but straight, eyes the colour of leaves on the creek bottom.

Hurrying over the leaves, a kind of shine.

Diner

She orders grilled cheese, I get
an omelet. She says, if you want to talk about—
aren't we all furred with it? We don't have long.
Look how time falls through the trees. She cries
when I get to the part about the shimmer.
I take her hand. The waitress
fills our cups, fills them so it's nearly impossible
to bring them to our mouths without
spilling.

We leave as one clustered hum, jostle
of passengers. Think of us
departing through frosted doors
into a life that lies beyond, that frisson of what can't be
seen—
what's next. Here we pause, together, alert
for the next instruction. Waiting,
we drift between the tines
of a cherry's branches. Tuning it
clear, sweet, once. Slipped, the slung warmth of each other,
uncertainty's buzz, poised, massed
into quiver. Chitchat of one body against another,
laddering under,
over, under, over. This is how we speak.
This is how we cling, unhived, undone: the was, the went.
Unkiltered, shuddered into the future. We dream
a many-chambered edifice of wax, honey-fragrant, rich
with our queen's babbled
brood, thousands a day. She is us.
Or she was. The whole thing's impossible
without her. We swarm
sharp-tanged bark,
blossoms fisted tight. Lashes
of rain to come. A few hours, that's all.

OTHERWORLD

Or the laddered
wing of a heron, blurred,
rising, the word for lifted.

Unlocked, whatever was locked. Ajar.

Scribbled curls of seaweed,
untethered ligature. Summered air, swim of tide.

Rose-dusked light,
necklace of beach, hour of not-quite. Wind, a breath,

cloudbrushed distance,
so unfolded it's almost gone. Wind to ocean, ocean to wind, wind to ocean.
Utterly
open,
as if you were

the word for open.

Each poem in the sequence called "The Drawings of Santiago Ramón y Cajal" is based on a drawing by the Spanish neuroanatomist Santiago Ramón y Cajal (1852-1934). I first saw a collection of his drawings in an exhibit called "The Beautiful Brain" at the Belkin Gallery, University of British Columbia, in 2017.

Gilgamesh is the first recorded literary work in the world. Stories about Gilgamesh, a pre-Sumerian king said to have lived in Uruk in present-day Iraq, and celebrated as a semi-divine figure, were written on tablets in the third millennium B.C. *Gilgamesh* tells of a profound and poignant friendship between the king, Gilgamesh, and the wild man, Enkidu, an inspiration for the two sequences—"I Take You" and "I Can't Take You"—included here.

The inspiration for "Spell" is from "Cloud Horses," a poem by Pat Lowther (*Time Capsule*, 1996).

The epigraph for "In Burlington" is from "Divine" (*Mortal Trash*, 2016) by Kim Addonizio.

"Someone Mentions *Woman Reading a Letter*" refers to a painting by Johannes Vermeer circa 1663.

"Strange Attractor" is inspired by the mathematical field of dynamical systems, in which attractors are a set of numerical values by which a system shapes itself. Strange attractors, though, exhibit unexpected or chaotic tendencies. While any dynamical system might not show coherence on a small scale—no variable can be duplicated, for instance—on a larger, global scale it may evolve in a way that reveals stability and order. "Strange Attractor" is a vision of a long marriage, a dynamical system involving two people.

"Impossible Staircase" is based on *Relativity* (1953) by M. C. Escher. The Penrose stairs, or impossible staircase, is a concept credited to Lionel Penrose and Roger Penrose, though prior to its discovery Roger Penrose was deeply influenced by the work of M. C. Escher.

"Test" is based on some of the questions from the Mini-Mental State Examination, a screening test for dementia.

"Taming the Bull" is based on one of the Ten Bulls of Zen Buddhism.

ACKNOWLEDGEMENTS

I am immensely grateful to the Canada Council and Arts Nova Scotia for support that allowed me time to write these poems.

Some of these poems were first published in *Hamilton Arts & Letters, Luminus, Paragon, Riddle Fence*, and *The Malahat Review*.

Excerpts of "Otherworld" were shown together with the landscape photographs of John Berridge at Lyghtesome Gallery in Antigonish, NS, in 2011. Many thanks to Beth and Jeff Parker. The full twelve-part text of "Otherworld" was also exhibited as part of *Gone*, together with a series of mixed media on vellum works—*Map of the Interior*—by artist Jane Everett. This exhibit was shown in 2014 at the Lake Country Art Gallery in Kelowna, BC, and in 2015 at the Carnegie Gallery in Dundas, ON. I am very grateful to Jane Everett.

The title poem for this book was written during the McLoughlin Gardens residency on Vancouver Island, BC, in 2016. My warmest thanks to Margo McLoughlin and her family.

Several poems—"Croton Leaf," "Grace," "Monkey Puzzle," and "Green Shine"—were written during a workshop given by Jane Hirshfield in Key West, FL, in 2015.

A number of poems were written at the abbey of the Trappistines in New Brunswick.

These poems were much improved because of the thoughtful attention given to them by Tonja Gunvaldsen Klaassen, best of readers.

To those fellow travellers I meet around the table in Burlington, much gratitude: Ross Belot, Dick Capling, Amy Dennis, Birgit Elston, and Donna McMurdo.

To everyone at McClelland & Stewart, thank you for your commitment to poetry. Warm thanks to Dionne Brand for her editing, and Kelly Joseph for her attention to every detail.

I am grateful for the loving support of my mother, Janet, my sisters, Jennifer and Susan, and their families, and especially my own wonderful family: Paul, David, and Sarah.

"Rachmaninoff's Prelude in G Major" is for Emily Logan.

"Party" is for Linda Clarke.

"Cup" is for Sky Wild Grady.

"The Drawings of Santiago Ramón y Cajal"—a poem sequence—is for Sarah Marquis.

"Monteverdi's Vespers" is in memory of Jordon Myles and Scott Cameron.

"Spell" is for Juniper Beatrice Frankland.

"Cake without Bride and Groom" is for Fiona Kinsella and Paul Lisson on the occasion
of their elopement.

"Barn" is for Kate Waters.

"Otherworld," originally one long poem, is in memory of Annette Ahern.

01 14

J